THIS BOOK BELONGS TO:

Bird Watching Journal for Kids

BeFoRe We GeT STaRTeD.....

LET'S LEARN ABOUT BIRDS

Birds are all over the world and they come in different sizes, shapes and colors.

 They are warm-blooded animals that reproduce by laying eggs, and most of them build nests to protect the eggs from weather and predators.

The main characteristic of a bird is

 **FEATHERS**

Birds are the only animals that have feathers.

Birds are **VERTEBRATES** (animals with backbones) that belong to a class or group named **"AVES"**

The word Aves means bird in Latin.

WHAT DO THEY EAT?

It depends on the type of bird, and the time of the year. Smaller birds usually eat seeds, worms, tiny insects; while bigger birds sometimes eat fish, eggs, and smaller animals.

Their **BEAKS** are adapted to help them grab and eat the food they need to survive. You can tell what a bird eats by looking at their beaks.

SEED-EATER
NECTAR-FEEDER
FISH-EATER
FRUIT & NUT-EATER
MEAT-EATER

HOW DO THEY FLY?

Birds fly by using their strong chest muscles to flap their wings with an up-and-down motion which pushes them forward. And their feathers adjust the airflow over and around the wings & body.

HOW DO THEY COMMUNICATE?

Birds communicate using sounds like: chirps, singing, squeaks, chirps, clicks, croaks, whistles and more.
Some birds also communicate by making sounds with their wings.
They usually communicate to claim territory, seek mates, ask for food, call their friends, and warn others about predators or any other type of danger.

MIGRATION

Every year, when the weather gets cold many birds make a long journey and fly to different areas looking for more food, warmer weather, and better conditions to have their babies. Birds are very smart, they use sun, the stars, and the earth's magnetism to figure out where to go. And then the next year as springtime approaches again, they will migrate back home.

BIRD BASICS

Learning about the body parts of a bird will help you describe them better and identify them a lot faster.
The illustration below shows the most basic parts of a bird:

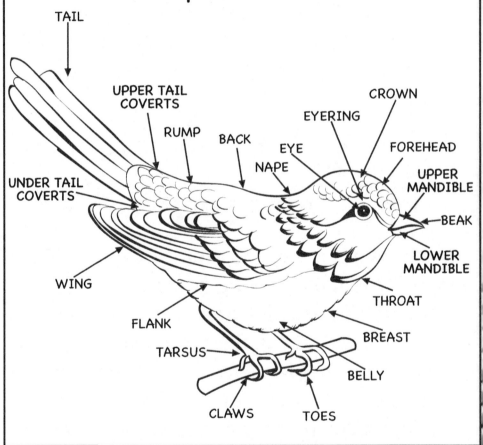

Birds are vertebrates, which means they have a spinal column (backbone) that support their bodies. Their bones are hollow, lightweight and strong; this allows them to fly and move easily through the air.
The illustration below shows what their skeleton looks like:

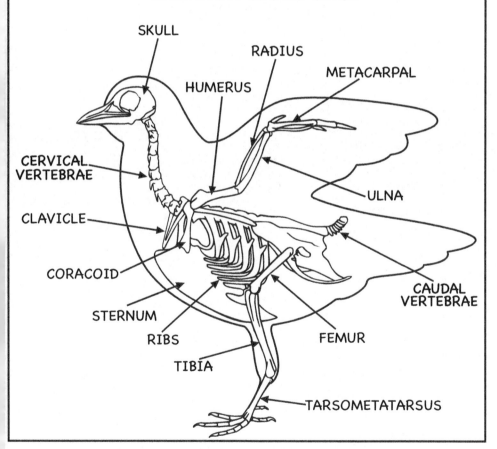

SKELETON OF A BIRD

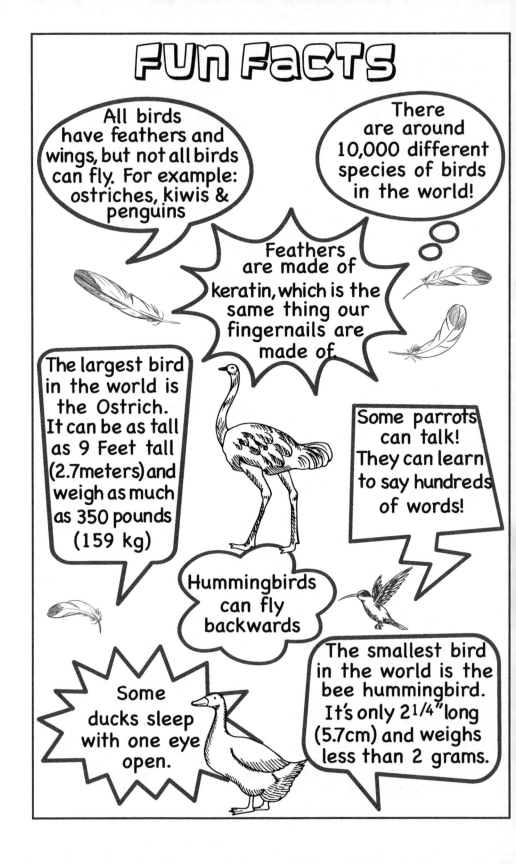

BIRD WATCHING

Bird watching can be a wonderful hobby for kids and adults. It can teach you how to be patient, focus, pay attention to details, and appreciate the beauty of nature and its wonderful creatures. It's also a good excuse to spend more time outdoors, and have a good time with friends or family.

GETTING STARTED...

You don't need to go far. Birds are found all across the world. You can find birds almost everywhere, even in your backyard or a public park in your neighborhood

Remember to use a field guide to help you identify the birds you see. If you don't have one you can also use the internet with the help of an adult. And last but not least, be patient and have lots of fun!!!

TIPS & TRICKS

FOLLOW THE CLUES

Look for signs such as bird poop, feathers, nests, eggs, or seeds. If you see these it means you're close!

LISTEN

Sometimes it's hard to spot birds, but it's easier to hear them. So if you can't spot any right away, try to be really quiet and listen carefully.

OBSERVE

If the birds are too far, you can use binoculars and spotting scopes to help you see them better!

CAPTURE THE MOMENT

Once you spot them, take a picture (or draw a quick sketch) before they fly away and then start taking notes on your journal (this book) and describe what you saw.

SHHHHH.....

Don't make any loud noises or sudden moves so you don't scare them away.

CHECKLIST

THESE ARE SOME THINGS YOU MAY WANT TO BRING ON A BIRD WATCH:

- [ ] Backpack
- [ ] Bug Spray & Sunscreen
- [ ] Water...Stay Hydrated!
- [ ] Healthy Snacks
- [ ] Binoculars or Spotting scopes
- [ ] Camera
- [ ] Field Guide: Local Bird Guide with pictures of the different species you may find in your area, to help you identify the birds you find.
- [ ] (This Book!) A Log Book or Journal to record your findings & observations
- [ ] Pencil and Eraser

NOW YOU ARE READY TO GO BIRDWATCHING! HAVE FUN!

BIRD WATCHING JOURNAL

DATE:	TIME:
WEATHER: ☀ ⛅ ☁ 🌧 ⛈ 🌙 ❄	SEASON: 🌸 ☀ 🍂 ❄
LOCATION:	

BIRD NAME:	BIRD TYPE:
HOW MANY DID YOU SEE? 1 2 3 4 5 6 7 8+	**HOW BIG IS THE BIRD?** Tiny Small Medium Big Very Big

BIRD LOCATION
- [ ] Ground
- [ ] Tree
- [ ] Air
- [ ] Bush
- [ ] Feeder
- [ ] Other_____

BEAK SHAPE
- [ ] Hooked
- [ ] Cone
- [ ] Pointy
- [ ] Flat
- [ ] Long
- [ ] Other_____

TAIL
- [ ] Short
- [ ] Long
- [ ] Straight
- [ ] Fanned
- [ ] Forked
- [ ] Other_____

WINGS SHAPE
- [ ] Short
- [ ] Long
- [ ] Pointy
- [ ] Broad
- [ ] Round
- [ ] Other_____

MARKINGS & COLORS
_____
_____
_____
_____

WHAT IS THE BIRD DOING?	DID THE BIRD SING?
_____ _____	☐ Yes ☐ No

OTHER INTERESTING THINGS I NOTICED

_____
_____
_____
_____
_____
_____

PHOTO / SKETCH

BIRD WATCHING JOURNAL

DATE:	**TIME:**
WEATHER: ☀ ⛅ ☁ 🌧 ⛈ 🌙 ❄	**SEASON:** ✿ ☀ 🍂 ❄
LOCATION:	

BIRD NAME:	**BIRD TYPE:**

HOW MANY DID YOU SEE?

1   2   3   4   5   6   7   8+

HOW BIG IS THE BIRD?

Tiny   Small   Medium   Big   Very Big

BIRD LOCATION
- ☐ Ground
- ☐ Tree
- ☐ Air
- ☐ Bush
- ☐ Feeder
- ☐ Other_____

BEAK SHAPE
- ☐ Hooked
- ☐ Cone
- ☐ Pointy
- ☐ Flat
- ☐ Long
- ☐ Other_____

TAIL
- ☐ Short
- ☐ Long
- ☐ Straight
- ☐ Fanned
- ☐ Forked
- ☐ Other_____

WINGS SHAPE
- ☐ Short
- ☐ Long
- ☐ Pointy
- ☐ Broad
- ☐ Round
- ☐ Other_____

MARKINGS & COLORS

_____

_____

_____

_____

WHAT IS THE BIRD DOING?

_____

_____

DID THE BIRD SING?

☐ Yes   ☐ No

OTHER INTERESTING THINGS I NOTICED

_____

_____

_____

_____

_____

_____

PHOTO / SKETCH

BIRD WATCHING JOURNAL

DATE:	TIME:
WEATHER: ☀️🌤️⛅☁️🌧️⛈️🌙❄️	**SEASON:** ✿ ☀️ 🍃 ❄️
LOCATION:	

BIRD NAME:	BIRD TYPE:
HOW MANY DID YOU SEE? 1 2 3 4 5 6 7 8+	**HOW BIG IS THE BIRD?** Tiny Small Medium Big Very Big

BIRD LOCATION
- ☐ Ground
- ☐ Tree
- ☐ Air
- ☐ Bush
- ☐ Feeder
- ☐ Other_____

BEAK SHAPE
- ☐ Hooked
- ☐ Cone
- ☐ Pointy
- ☐ Flat
- ☐ Long
- ☐ Other_____

TAIL
- ☐ Short
- ☐ Long
- ☐ Straight
- ☐ Fanned
- ☐ Forked
- ☐ Other_____

WINGS SHAPE
- ☐ Short
- ☐ Long
- ☐ Pointy
- ☐ Broad
- ☐ Round
- ☐ Other_____

MARKINGS & COLORS

_____

_____

_____

_____

WHAT IS THE BIRD DOING?

_____

_____

DID THE BIRD SING?

☐ Yes   ☐ No

OTHER INTERESTING THINGS I NOTICED

_____

_____

_____

_____

_____

_____

PHOTO / SKETCH

BIRD WATCHING JOURNAL

DATE:	TIME:
WEATHER: ☀ ⛅ ☁ 🌧 🌦 🌙 ❄	SEASON: ✿ ☀ 🍃 ❄
LOCATION:	

BIRD NAME:	BIRD TYPE:
HOW MANY DID YOU SEE? 1 2 3 4 5 6 7 8+	**HOW BIG IS THE BIRD?** Tiny Small Medium Big Very Big

BIRD LOCATION
- ☐ Ground
- ☐ Tree
- ☐ Air
- ☐ Bush
- ☐ Feeder
- ☐ Other_____

BEAK SHAPE
- ☐ Hooked
- ☐ Cone
- ☐ Pointy
- ☐ Flat
- ☐ Long
- ☐ Other_____

TAIL
- ☐ Short
- ☐ Long
- ☐ Straight
- ☐ Fanned
- ☐ Forked
- ☐ Other_____

WINGS SHAPE
- ☐ Short
- ☐ Long
- ☐ Pointy
- ☐ Broad
- ☐ Round
- ☐ Other_____

MARKINGS & COLORS
_____
_____
_____
_____

WHAT IS THE BIRD DOING?

_____

_____

DID THE BIRD SING?

☐ Yes   ☐ No

OTHER INTERESTING THINGS I NOTICED

_____

_____

_____

_____

_____

_____

PHOTO / SKETCH

BIRD WATCHING JOURNAL

DATE:

TIME:

WEATHER: ☀ ⛅ ☁ ☁ 🌧 ⛈ 🌙 ❄

SEASON: ✿ ☀ 🍃 ❄

LOCATION:

BIRD NAME:	**BIRD TYPE:**

HOW MANY DID YOU SEE?

1   2   3   4   5   6   7   8+

HOW BIG IS THE BIRD?

Tiny   Small   Medium   Big   Very Big

BIRD LOCATION
- [ ] Ground
- [ ] Tree
- [ ] Air
- [ ] Bush
- [ ] Feeder
- [ ] Other_____

BEAK SHAPE
- [ ] Hooked
- [ ] Cone
- [ ] Pointy
- [ ] Flat
- [ ] Long
- [ ] Other_____

TAIL
- [ ] Short
- [ ] Long
- [ ] Straight
- [ ] Fanned
- [ ] Forked
- [ ] Other_____

WINGS SHAPE
- [ ] Short
- [ ] Long
- [ ] Pointy
- [ ] Broad
- [ ] Round
- [ ] Other_____

MARKINGS & COLORS

_____

_____

_____

_____

WHAT IS THE BIRD DOING?

_____

_____

DID THE BIRD SING?

☐ Yes   ☐ No

OTHER INTERESTING THINGS I NOTICED

_____

_____

_____

_____

_____

PHOTO / SKETCH

BIRD WATCHING JOURNAL

DATE:	**TIME:**
WEATHER: ☀️🌤️⛅🌧️⛈️🌙❄️	**SEASON:** 🌸 ☀️ 🍂 ❄️
LOCATION:	

BIRD NAME:	**BIRD TYPE:**
HOW MANY DID YOU SEE? 1 2 3 4 5 6 7 8+	**HOW BIG IS THE BIRD?** Tiny Small Medium Big Very Big

BIRD LOCATION
- [ ] Ground
- [ ] Tree
- [ ] Air
- [ ] Bush
- [ ] Feeder
- [ ] Other_____

BEAK SHAPE
- [ ] Hooked
- [ ] Cone
- [ ] Pointy
- [ ] Flat
- [ ] Long
- [ ] Other_____

TAIL
- [ ] Short
- [ ] Long
- [ ] Straight
- [ ] Fanned
- [ ] Forked
- [ ] Other_____

WINGS SHAPE
- [ ] Short
- [ ] Long
- [ ] Pointy
- [ ] Broad
- [ ] Round
- [ ] Other_____

MARKINGS & COLORS

_____

_____

_____

_____

WHAT IS THE BIRD DOING?

_____

_____

DID THE BIRD SING?

☐ Yes　　☐ No

OTHER INTERESTING THINGS I NOTICED

_____

_____

_____

_____

_____

_____

PHOTO / SKETCH

BIRD WATCHING JOURNAL

DATE:	TIME:
WEATHER:☀️⛅☁️🌧️⛈️🌙❄️	SEASON: 🌸 ☀️ 🍂 ❄️
LOCATION:	

BIRD NAME:	BIRD TYPE:
HOW MANY DID YOU SEE? 1 2 3 4 5 6 7 8+	**HOW BIG IS THE BIRD?** Tiny Small Medium Big Very Big

BIRD LOCATION
- ☐ Ground
- ☐ Tree
- ☐ Air
- ☐ Bush
- ☐ Feeder
- ☐ Other_____

BEAK SHAPE
- ☐ Hooked
- ☐ Cone
- ☐ Pointy
- ☐ Flat
- ☐ Long
- ☐ Other_____

TAIL
- ☐ Short
- ☐ Long
- ☐ Straight
- ☐ Fanned
- ☐ Forked
- ☐ Other_____

WINGS SHAPE
- ☐ Short
- ☐ Long
- ☐ Pointy
- ☐ Broad
- ☐ Round
- ☐ Other_____

MARKINGS & COLORS

_____

_____

_____

_____

WHAT IS THE BIRD DOING?

_____

_____

DID THE BIRD SING?

☐ Yes   ☐ No

OTHER INTERESTING THINGS I NOTICED

_____

_____

_____

_____

_____

_____

PHOTO / SKETCH

BIRD WATCHING JOURNAL

DATE:

TIME:

WEATHER:

SEASON:

LOCATION:

BIRD NAME:

BIRD TYPE:

HOW MANY DID YOU SEE?

1   2   3   4   5   6   7   8+

HOW BIG IS THE BIRD?

Tiny   Small   Medium   Big   Very Big

BIRD LOCATION
- [ ] Ground
- [ ] Tree
- [ ] Air
- [ ] Bush
- [ ] Feeder
- [ ] Other_____

BEAK SHAPE
- [ ] Hooked
- [ ] Cone
- [ ] Pointy
- [ ] Flat
- [ ] Long
- [ ] Other_____

TAIL
- [ ] Short
- [ ] Long
- [ ] Straight
- [ ] Fanned
- [ ] Forked
- [ ] Other_____

WINGS SHAPE
- [ ] Short
- [ ] Long
- [ ] Pointy
- [ ] Broad
- [ ] Round
- [ ] Other_____

MARKINGS & COLORS

_____

_____

_____

_____

WHAT IS THE BIRD DOING?

_____

_____

DID THE BIRD SING?

☐ Yes   ☐ No

OTHER INTERESTING THINGS I NOTICED

_____

_____

_____

_____

_____

_____

PHOTO / SKETCH

BIRD WATCHING JOURNAL

DATE:	TIME:
WEATHER: ☀️🌤️⛅🌧️⛈️🌙❄️	SEASON: 🌸 ☀️ 🍂 ❄️
LOCATION:	

BIRD NAME:	BIRD TYPE:
HOW MANY DID YOU SEE? 1 2 3 4 5 6 7 8+	**HOW BIG IS THE BIRD?** Tiny Small Medium Big Very Big

BIRD LOCATION
- ☐ Ground
- ☐ Tree
- ☐ Air
- ☐ Bush
- ☐ Feeder
- ☐ Other_____

BEAK SHAPE
- ☐ Hooked
- ☐ Cone
- ☐ Pointy
- ☐ Flat
- ☐ Long
- ☐ Other_____

TAIL
- ☐ Short
- ☐ Long
- ☐ Straight
- ☐ Fanned
- ☐ Forked
- ☐ Other_____

WINGS SHAPE
- ☐ Short
- ☐ Long
- ☐ Pointy
- ☐ Broad
- ☐ Round
- ☐ Other_____

MARKINGS & COLORS

_____

_____

_____

_____

WHAT IS THE BIRD DOING?

_____

_____

DID THE BIRD SING?

☐ Yes   ☐ No

OTHER INTERESTING THINGS I NOTICED

_____

_____

_____

_____

_____

_____

PHOTO / SKETCH

BIRD WATCHING JOURNAL

DATE:	TIME:
WEATHER: ☀️🌤️☁️⛅🌧️⛈️🌙❄️	SEASON: ✿ ☀️ 🍂 ❄️
LOCATION:	

BIRD NAME:	BIRD TYPE:
HOW MANY DID YOU SEE? 1 2 3 4 5 6 7 8+	**HOW BIG IS THE BIRD?** Tiny Small Medium Big Very Big

BIRD LOCATION
- [ ] Ground
- [ ] Tree
- [ ] Air
- [ ] Bush
- [ ] Feeder
- [ ] Other_____

BEAK SHAPE
- [ ] Hooked
- [ ] Cone
- [ ] Pointy
- [ ] Flat
- [ ] Long
- [ ] Other_____

TAIL
- [ ] Short
- [ ] Long
- [ ] Straight
- [ ] Fanned
- [ ] Forked
- [ ] Other_____

WINGS SHAPE
- [ ] Short
- [ ] Long
- [ ] Pointy
- [ ] Broad
- [ ] Round
- [ ] Other_____

MARKINGS & COLORS
_____
_____
_____
_____

WHAT IS THE BIRD DOING?

_____

_____

DID THE BIRD SING?

☐ Yes   ☐ No

OTHER INTERESTING THINGS I NOTICED

_____

_____

_____

_____

_____

_____

PHOTO / SKETCH

BIRD WATCHING JOURNAL

DATE:	TIME:
WEATHER: ☀️🌤️☁️🌧️⛈️🌙❄️	SEASON: ✿ ☀️ 🍂 ❄️
LOCATION:	

BIRD NAME:	BIRD TYPE:
HOW MANY DID YOU SEE? 1 2 3 4 5 6 7 8+	**HOW BIG IS THE BIRD?** Tiny Small Medium Big Very Big

BIRD LOCATION
- [ ] Ground
- [ ] Tree
- [ ] Air
- [ ] Bush
- [ ] Feeder
- [ ] Other_____

BEAK SHAPE
- [ ] Hooked
- [ ] Cone
- [ ] Pointy
- [ ] Flat
- [ ] Long
- [ ] Other_____

TAIL
- [ ] Short
- [ ] Long
- [ ] Straight
- [ ] Fanned
- [ ] Forked
- [ ] Other_____

WINGS SHAPE
- [ ] Short
- [ ] Long
- [ ] Pointy
- [ ] Broad
- [ ] Round
- [ ] Other_____

MARKINGS & COLORS

_____
_____
_____
_____

WHAT IS THE BIRD DOING?

_____

_____

DID THE BIRD SING?

☐ Yes   ☐ No

OTHER INTERESTING THINGS I NOTICED

_____

_____

_____

_____

_____

_____

PHOTO / SKETCH

BIRD WATCHING JOURNAL

DATE:	TIME:
WEATHER: ☀️⛅☁️🌧️⛈️🌙❄️	SEASON: ✿ ☀️ 🍃 ❄️
LOCATION:	

BIRD NAME:	BIRD TYPE:
HOW MANY DID YOU SEE? 1 2 3 4 5 6 7 8+	**HOW BIG IS THE BIRD?** Tiny Small Medium Big Very Big

BIRD LOCATION
- ☐ Ground
- ☐ Tree
- ☐ Air
- ☐ Bush
- ☐ Feeder
- ☐ Other_____

BEAK SHAPE
- ☐ Hooked
- ☐ Cone
- ☐ Pointy
- ☐ Flat
- ☐ Long
- ☐ Other_____

TAIL
- ☐ Short
- ☐ Long
- ☐ Straight
- ☐ Fanned
- ☐ Forked
- ☐ Other_____

WINGS SHAPE
- ☐ Short
- ☐ Long
- ☐ Pointy
- ☐ Broad
- ☐ Round
- ☐ Other_____

MARKINGS & COLORS

_____
_____
_____
_____

WHAT IS THE BIRD DOING?

_____

_____

DID THE BIRD SING?

☐ Yes   ☐ No

OTHER INTERESTING THINGS I NOTICED

_____

_____

_____

_____

_____

_____

PHOTO / SKETCH

BIRD WATCHING JOURNAL

DATE:	TIME:
WEATHER: ☀☁☁☁☁☾❄	SEASON: ✿ ☀ 🍂 ❄
LOCATION:	

BIRD NAME:	BIRD TYPE:
HOW MANY DID YOU SEE? 1 2 3 4 5 6 7 8+	**HOW BIG IS THE BIRD?** Tiny Small Medium Big Very Big

BIRD LOCATION
- ☐ Ground
- ☐ Tree
- ☐ Air
- ☐ Bush
- ☐ Feeder
- ☐ Other _____

BEAK SHAPE
- ☐ Hooked
- ☐ Cone
- ☐ Pointy
- ☐ Flat
- ☐ Long
- ☐ Other _____

TAIL
- ☐ Short
- ☐ Long
- ☐ Straight
- ☐ Fanned
- ☐ Forked
- ☐ Other _____

WINGS SHAPE
- ☐ Short
- ☐ Long
- ☐ Pointy
- ☐ Broad
- ☐ Round
- ☐ Other _____

MARKINGS & COLORS

_____

_____

_____

_____

WHAT IS THE BIRD DOING?

_____

_____

DID THE BIRD SING?

☐ Yes   ☐ No

OTHER INTERESTING THINGS I NOTICED

_____

_____

_____

_____

_____

_____

PHOTO / SKETCH

BIRD WATCHING JOURNAL

DATE:	TIME:
WEATHER: ☀☁☁☁☁🌙❄	SEASON: ✿ ☀ 🍃 ❄
LOCATION:	

BIRD NAME:	BIRD TYPE:
HOW MANY DID YOU SEE? 1 2 3 4 5 6 7 8+	**HOW BIG IS THE BIRD?** Tiny Small Medium Big Very Big

BIRD LOCATION
- [ ] Ground
- [ ] Tree
- [ ] Air
- [ ] Bush
- [ ] Feeder
- [ ] Other_____

BEAK SHAPE
- [ ] Hooked
- [ ] Cone
- [ ] Pointy
- [ ] Flat
- [ ] Long
- [ ] Other_____

TAIL
- [ ] Short
- [ ] Long
- [ ] Straight
- [ ] Fanned
- [ ] Forked
- [ ] Other_____

WINGS SHAPE
- [ ] Short
- [ ] Long
- [ ] Pointy
- [ ] Broad
- [ ] Round
- [ ] Other_____

MARKINGS & COLORS

_____
_____
_____
_____

WHAT IS THE BIRD DOING?

_____

_____

DID THE BIRD SING?

☐ Yes   ☐ No

OTHER INTERESTING THINGS I NOTICED

_____

_____

_____

_____

_____

_____

PHOTO / SKETCH

BIRD WATCHING JOURNAL

DATE:	TIME:
WEATHER: ☀️🌤️☁️🌧️⛈️🌙❄️	**SEASON:** ✿ ☀ 🍂 ❄️
LOCATION:	

BIRD NAME:	BIRD TYPE:
HOW MANY DID YOU SEE? 1 2 3 4 5 6 7 8+	**HOW BIG IS THE BIRD?** Tiny Small Medium Big Very Big

BIRD LOCATION
- ☐ Ground
- ☐ Tree
- ☐ Air
- ☐ Bush
- ☐ Feeder
- ☐ Other_____

BEAK SHAPE
- ☐ Hooked
- ☐ Cone
- ☐ Pointy
- ☐ Flat
- ☐ Long
- ☐ Other_____

TAIL
- ☐ Short
- ☐ Long
- ☐ Straight
- ☐ Fanned
- ☐ Forked
- ☐ Other_____

WINGS SHAPE
- ☐ Short
- ☐ Long
- ☐ Pointy
- ☐ Broad
- ☐ Round
- ☐ Other_____

MARKINGS & COLORS

_____
_____
_____
_____

WHAT IS THE BIRD DOING?

_____

_____

DID THE BIRD SING?

☐ Yes   ☐ No

OTHER INTERESTING THINGS I NOTICED

_____

_____

_____

_____

_____

_____

PHOTO / SKETCH

BIRD WATCHING JOURNAL

DATE:

TIME:

WEATHER:

SEASON:

LOCATION:

BIRD NAME:

BIRD TYPE:

HOW MANY DID YOU SEE?

1   2   3   4   5   6   7   8+

HOW BIG IS THE BIRD?

Tiny   Small   Medium   Big   Very Big

BIRD LOCATION
- [ ] Ground
- [ ] Tree
- [ ] Air
- [ ] Bush
- [ ] Feeder
- [ ] Other_____

BEAK SHAPE
- [ ] Hooked
- [ ] Cone
- [ ] Pointy
- [ ] Flat
- [ ] Long
- [ ] Other_____

TAIL
- [ ] Short
- [ ] Long
- [ ] Straight
- [ ] Fanned
- [ ] Forked
- [ ] Other_____

WINGS SHAPE
- [ ] Short
- [ ] Long
- [ ] Pointy
- [ ] Broad
- [ ] Round
- [ ] Other_____

MARKINGS & COLORS

_____

_____

_____

_____

WHAT IS THE BIRD DOING?

_____

_____

DID THE BIRD SING?

☐ Yes ☐ No

OTHER INTERESTING THINGS I NOTICED

_____

_____

_____

_____

_____

_____

PHOTO / SKETCH

BIRD WATCHING JOURNAL

DATE:	TIME:
WEATHER: ☀️🌤️⛅☁️🌧️⛈️🌙❄️	SEASON: ✿ ☀️ 🍂 ❄️
LOCATION:	

BIRD NAME:	BIRD TYPE:
HOW MANY DID YOU SEE? 1 2 3 4 5 6 7 8+	**HOW BIG IS THE BIRD?** Tiny Small Medium Big Very Big

BIRD LOCATION
- ☐ Ground
- ☐ Tree
- ☐ Air
- ☐ Bush
- ☐ Feeder
- ☐ Other_____

BEAK SHAPE
- ☐ Hooked
- ☐ Cone
- ☐ Pointy
- ☐ Flat
- ☐ Long
- ☐ Other_____

TAIL
- ☐ Short
- ☐ Long
- ☐ Straight
- ☐ Fanned
- ☐ Forked
- ☐ Other_____

WINGS SHAPE
- ☐ Short
- ☐ Long
- ☐ Pointy
- ☐ Broad
- ☐ Round
- ☐ Other_____

MARKINGS & COLORS

_____

_____

_____

_____

WHAT IS THE BIRD DOING?

_____

_____

DID THE BIRD SING?

☐ Yes   ☐ No

OTHER INTERESTING THINGS I NOTICED

_____

_____

_____

_____

_____

_____

PHOTO / SKETCH

BIRD WATCHING JOURNAL

DATE:	TIME:
WEATHER: ☀️⛅☁️🌦️⛈️🌙❄️	SEASON: 🌸 ☀️ 🍂 ❄️
LOCATION:	

BIRD NAME:	BIRD TYPE:
HOW MANY DID YOU SEE? 1 2 3 4 5 6 7 8+	**HOW BIG IS THE BIRD?** Tiny Small Medium Big Very Big

BIRD LOCATION
- ☐ Ground
- ☐ Tree
- ☐ Air
- ☐ Bush
- ☐ Feeder
- ☐ Other_____

BEAK SHAPE
- ☐ Hooked
- ☐ Cone
- ☐ Pointy
- ☐ Flat
- ☐ Long
- ☐ Other_____

TAIL
- ☐ Short
- ☐ Long
- ☐ Straight
- ☐ Fanned
- ☐ Forked
- ☐ Other_____

WINGS SHAPE
- ☐ Short
- ☐ Long
- ☐ Pointy
- ☐ Broad
- ☐ Round
- ☐ Other_____

MARKINGS & COLORS

_____
_____
_____
_____

WHAT IS THE BIRD DOING?

_____

_____

DID THE BIRD SING?

☐ Yes   ☐ No

OTHER INTERESTING THINGS I NOTICED

_____

_____

_____

_____

_____

_____

PHOTO / SKETCH

BIRD WATCHING JOURNAL

DATE:	TIME:
WEATHER: ☀☁☁☁☁🌙❄	SEASON: ❀ ☀ 🌱 ❄
LOCATION:	

BIRD NAME:	BIRD TYPE:
HOW MANY DID YOU SEE? 1 2 3 4 5 6 7 8+	**HOW BIG IS THE BIRD?** Tiny Small Medium Big Very Big

BIRD LOCATION
- [ ] Ground
- [ ] Tree
- [ ] Air
- [ ] Bush
- [ ] Feeder
- [ ] Other_____

BEAK SHAPE
- [ ] Hooked
- [ ] Cone
- [ ] Pointy
- [ ] Flat
- [ ] Long
- [ ] Other_____

TAIL
- [ ] Short
- [ ] Long
- [ ] Straight
- [ ] Fanned
- [ ] Forked
- [ ] Other_____

WINGS SHAPE
- [ ] Short
- [ ] Long
- [ ] Pointy
- [ ] Broad
- [ ] Round
- [ ] Other_____

MARKINGS & COLORS

_____
_____
_____
_____

WHAT IS THE BIRD DOING?

_____

_____

DID THE BIRD SING?

☐ Yes   ☐ No

OTHER INTERESTING THINGS I NOTICED

_____

_____

_____

_____

_____

_____

PHOTO / SKETCH

BIRD WATCHING JOURNAL

DATE:	TIME:

WEATHER: ☀☁⛅☁🌧⛈🌙❄ **SEASON:** ✿ ☀ 🍃 ❄

LOCATION:

BIRD NAME:	BIRD TYPE:

HOW MANY DID YOU SEE?

1 2 3 4 5 6 7 8+

HOW BIG IS THE BIRD?

Tiny Small Medium Big Very Big

BIRD LOCATION
- ☐ Ground
- ☐ Tree
- ☐ Air
- ☐ Bush
- ☐ Feeder
- ☐ Other_____

BEAK SHAPE
- ☐ Hooked
- ☐ Cone
- ☐ Pointy
- ☐ Flat
- ☐ Long
- ☐ Other_____

TAIL
- ☐ Short
- ☐ Long
- ☐ Straight
- ☐ Fanned
- ☐ Forked
- ☐ Other_____

WINGS SHAPE
- ☐ Short
- ☐ Long
- ☐ Pointy
- ☐ Broad
- ☐ Round
- ☐ Other_____

MARKINGS & COLORS

_____

_____

_____

_____

WHAT IS THE BIRD DOING?

_____

_____

DID THE BIRD SING?

☐ Yes   ☐ No

OTHER INTERESTING THINGS I NOTICED

_____

_____

_____

_____

_____

_____

PHOTO / SKETCH

BIRD WATCHING JOURNAL

DATE:	**TIME:**
WEATHER: ☀️🌤️☁️🌦️🌧️🌙❄️	**SEASON:** ✿ ☀️ 🍃 ❄️
LOCATION:	

BIRD NAME:	**BIRD TYPE:**
HOW MANY DID YOU SEE? 1 2 3 4 5 6 7 8+	**HOW BIG IS THE BIRD?** Tiny Small Medium Big Very Big

BIRD LOCATION
- [ ] Ground
- [ ] Tree
- [ ] Air
- [ ] Bush
- [ ] Feeder
- [ ] Other _____

BEAK SHAPE
- [ ] Hooked
- [ ] Cone
- [ ] Pointy
- [ ] Flat
- [ ] Long
- [ ] Other _____

TAIL
- [ ] Short
- [ ] Long
- [ ] Straight
- [ ] Fanned
- [ ] Forked
- [ ] Other _____

WINGS SHAPE
- [ ] Short
- [ ] Long
- [ ] Pointy
- [ ] Broad
- [ ] Round
- [ ] Other _____

MARKINGS & COLORS

_____

_____

_____

_____

WHAT IS THE BIRD DOING?

_____

_____

DID THE BIRD SING?

☐ Yes   ☐ No

OTHER INTERESTING THINGS I NOTICED

_____

_____

_____

_____

_____

_____

PHOTO / SKETCH

BIRD WATCHING JOURNAL

DATE:	TIME:
WEATHER: ☀️🌤️☁️🌧️⛈️🌙❄️	**SEASON:** ❀ ☀️ 🍃 ❄️
LOCATION:	

BIRD NAME:	BIRD TYPE:
HOW MANY DID YOU SEE? 1 2 3 4 5 6 7 8+	**HOW BIG IS THE BIRD?** Tiny Small Medium Big Very Big

BIRD LOCATION
- ☐ Ground
- ☐ Tree
- ☐ Air
- ☐ Bush
- ☐ Feeder
- ☐ Other_____

BEAK SHAPE
- ☐ Hooked
- ☐ Cone
- ☐ Pointy
- ☐ Flat
- ☐ Long
- ☐ Other_____

TAIL
- ☐ Short
- ☐ Long
- ☐ Straight
- ☐ Fanned
- ☐ Forked
- ☐ Other_____

WINGS SHAPE
- ☐ Short
- ☐ Long
- ☐ Pointy
- ☐ Broad
- ☐ Round
- ☐ Other_____

MARKINGS & COLORS

_____
_____
_____
_____

WHAT IS THE BIRD DOING?

_____

_____

DID THE BIRD SING?

☐ Yes   ☐ No

OTHER INTERESTING THINGS I NOTICED

_____

_____

_____

_____

_____

_____

PHOTO / SKETCH

BIRD WATCHING JOURNAL

DATE:

TIME:

WEATHER:

SEASON:

LOCATION:

BIRD NAME:

BIRD TYPE:

HOW MANY DID YOU SEE?

1   2   3   4   5   6   7   8+

HOW BIG IS THE BIRD?

Tiny   Small   Medium   Big   Very Big

BIRD LOCATION

☐ Ground
☐ Tree
☐ Air
☐ Bush
☐ Feeder
☐ Other_____

BEAK SHAPE

☐ Hooked
☐ Cone
☐ Pointy
☐ Flat
☐ Long
☐ Other_____

TAIL

☐ Short
☐ Long
☐ Straight
☐ Fanned
☐ Forked
☐ Other_____

WINGS SHAPE

☐ Short
☐ Long
☐ Pointy
☐ Broad
☐ Round
☐ Other_____

MARKINGS & COLORS

_____

_____

_____

_____

WHAT IS THE BIRD DOING?

_____

_____

DID THE BIRD SING?

☐ Yes   ☐ No

OTHER INTERESTING THINGS I NOTICED

_____

_____

_____

_____

_____

_____

PHOTO / SKETCH

BIRD WATCHING JOURNAL

DATE:	TIME:
WEATHER: ☀🌤☁🌦🌧🌙❄	SEASON: ✿ ☀ 🍂 ❄
LOCATION:	

BIRD NAME:	BIRD TYPE:
HOW MANY DID YOU SEE? 1　2　3　4　5　6　7　8+	**HOW BIG IS THE BIRD?** Tiny　Small　Medium　Big　Very Big

BIRD LOCATION
- ☐ Ground
- ☐ Tree
- ☐ Air
- ☐ Bush
- ☐ Feeder
- ☐ Other _____

BEAK SHAPE
- ☐ Hooked
- ☐ Cone
- ☐ Pointy
- ☐ Flat
- ☐ Long
- ☐ Other _____

TAIL
- ☐ Short
- ☐ Long
- ☐ Straight
- ☐ Fanned
- ☐ Forked
- ☐ Other _____

WINGS SHAPE
- ☐ Short
- ☐ Long
- ☐ Pointy
- ☐ Broad
- ☐ Round
- ☐ Other _____

MARKINGS & COLORS

_____

_____

_____

_____

WHAT IS THE BIRD DOING?

_____

_____

DID THE BIRD SING?

☐ Yes ☐ No

OTHER INTERESTING THINGS I NOTICED

_____

_____

_____

_____

_____

_____

PHOTO / SKETCH

BIRD WATCHING JOURNAL

DATE:	TIME:
WEATHER: ☀🌤☁⛅🌧⛈🌙❄	SEASON: ❀ ☀ 🍃 ❄
LOCATION:	

BIRD NAME:	BIRD TYPE:

HOW MANY DID YOU SEE?	HOW BIG IS THE BIRD?
1 2 3 4 5 6 7 8+	Tiny Small Medium Big Very Big

BIRD LOCATION
- ☐ Ground
- ☐ Tree
- ☐ Air
- ☐ Bush
- ☐ Feeder
- ☐ Other_____

BEAK SHAPE
- ☐ Hooked
- ☐ Cone
- ☐ Pointy
- ☐ Flat
- ☐ Long
- ☐ Other_____

TAIL
- ☐ Short
- ☐ Long
- ☐ Straight
- ☐ Fanned
- ☐ Forked
- ☐ Other_____

WINGS SHAPE
- ☐ Short
- ☐ Long
- ☐ Pointy
- ☐ Broad
- ☐ Round
- ☐ Other_____

MARKINGS & COLORS

_____

_____

_____

_____

WHAT IS THE BIRD DOING?

_____

_____

DID THE BIRD SING?

☐ Yes   ☐ No

OTHER INTERESTING THINGS I NOTICED

_____

_____

_____

_____

_____

_____

PHOTO / SKETCH

BIRD WATCHING JOURNAL

DATE: **TIME:**

WEATHER: ☀️🌤️☁️🌧️⛈️🌙❄️   **SEASON:** 🌸 ☀️ 🍃 ❄️

LOCATION:

BIRD NAME: **BIRD TYPE:**

HOW MANY DID YOU SEE?   **HOW BIG IS THE BIRD?**

1   2   3   4   5   6   7   8+   Tiny Small Medium Big Very Big

BIRD LOCATION
- ☐ Ground
- ☐ Tree
- ☐ Air
- ☐ Bush
- ☐ Feeder
- ☐ Other_____

BEAK SHAPE
- ☐ Hooked
- ☐ Cone
- ☐ Pointy
- ☐ Flat
- ☐ Long
- ☐ Other_____

TAIL
- ☐ Short
- ☐ Long
- ☐ Straight
- ☐ Fanned
- ☐ Forked
- ☐ Other_____

WINGS SHAPE
- ☐ Short
- ☐ Long
- ☐ Pointy
- ☐ Broad
- ☐ Round
- ☐ Other_____

MARKINGS & COLORS

_____

_____

_____

_____

WHAT IS THE BIRD DOING?

_____

_____

DID THE BIRD SING?

☐ Yes   ☐ No

OTHER INTERESTING THINGS I NOTICED

_____

_____

_____

_____

_____

_____

PHOTO / SKETCH

BIRD WATCHING JOURNAL

DATE:	**TIME:**
WEATHER: ☀️🌤️⛅☁️🌦️🌧️🌙❄️	**SEASON:** 🌸 ☀️ 🍃 ❄️
LOCATION:	

BIRD NAME:	**BIRD TYPE:**
HOW MANY DID YOU SEE? 1　2　3　4　5　6　7　8+	**HOW BIG IS THE BIRD?** Tiny　Small　Medium　Big　Very Big

---

BIRD LOCATION
- ☐ Ground
- ☐ Tree
- ☐ Air
- ☐ Bush
- ☐ Feeder
- ☐ Other _____

BEAK SHAPE
- ☐ Hooked
- ☐ Cone
- ☐ Pointy
- ☐ Flat
- ☐ Long
- ☐ Other _____

TAIL
- ☐ Short
- ☐ Long
- ☐ Straight
- ☐ Fanned
- ☐ Forked
- ☐ Other _____

WINGS SHAPE
- ☐ Short
- ☐ Long
- ☐ Pointy
- ☐ Broad
- ☐ Round
- ☐ Other _____

MARKINGS & COLORS

_____

_____

_____

_____

WHAT IS THE BIRD DOING?

_____

_____

DID THE BIRD SING?

☐ Yes   ☐ No

OTHER INTERESTING THINGS I NOTICED

_____

_____

_____

_____

_____

_____

PHOTO / SKETCH

BIRD WATCHING JOURNAL

DATE:	TIME:
WEATHER: ☀☁☁☁☁☁☾❄	SEASON: ❀ ☀ 🍂 ❄
LOCATION:	

BIRD NAME:	BIRD TYPE:
HOW MANY DID YOU SEE? 1 2 3 4 5 6 7 8+	**HOW BIG IS THE BIRD?** Tiny Small Medium Big Very Big

BIRD LOCATION	BEAK SHAPE
☐ Ground	☐ Hooked
☐ Tree	☐ Cone
☐ Air	☐ Pointy
☐ Bush	☐ Flat
☐ Feeder	☐ Long
☐ Other_____	☐ Other_____

TAIL	WINGS SHAPE
☐ Short	☐ Short
☐ Long	☐ Long
☐ Straight	☐ Pointy
☐ Fanned	☐ Broad
☐ Forked	☐ Round
☐ Other_____	☐ Other_____

MARKINGS & COLORS

_____

_____

_____

_____

WHAT IS THE BIRD DOING?

_____

_____

DID THE BIRD SING?

☐ Yes   ☐ No

OTHER INTERESTING THINGS I NOTICED

_____

_____

_____

_____

_____

_____

PHOTO / SKETCH

BIRD WATCHING JOURNAL

DATE:	TIME:
WEATHER: ☀️🌤️☁️🌧️⛈️🌙❄️	SEASON: ✿ ☀️ 🍃 ❄️
LOCATION:	

BIRD NAME:	BIRD TYPE:
HOW MANY DID YOU SEE? 1 2 3 4 5 6 7 8+	**HOW BIG IS THE BIRD?** Tiny Small Medium Big Very Big

BIRD LOCATION
- ☐ Ground
- ☐ Tree
- ☐ Air
- ☐ Bush
- ☐ Feeder
- ☐ Other_____

BEAK SHAPE
- ☐ Hooked
- ☐ Cone
- ☐ Pointy
- ☐ Flat
- ☐ Long
- ☐ Other_____

TAIL
- ☐ Short
- ☐ Long
- ☐ Straight
- ☐ Fanned
- ☐ Forked
- ☐ Other_____

WINGS SHAPE
- ☐ Short
- ☐ Long
- ☐ Pointy
- ☐ Broad
- ☐ Round
- ☐ Other_____

MARKINGS & COLORS
_____
_____
_____
_____

WHAT IS THE BIRD DOING?

_____

_____

DID THE BIRD SING?

☐ Yes   ☐ No

OTHER INTERESTING THINGS I NOTICED

_____

_____

_____

_____

_____

_____

PHOTO / SKETCH

BIRD WATCHING JOURNAL

DATE:	TIME:
WEATHER: ☀🌤⛅🌧⛈🌙❄	SEASON: ✿ ☀ 🍂 ❄
LOCATION:	

BIRD NAME:	BIRD TYPE:
HOW MANY DID YOU SEE? 1 2 3 4 5 6 7 8+	**HOW BIG IS THE BIRD?** Tiny Small Medium Big Very Big

BIRD LOCATION
- ☐ Ground
- ☐ Tree
- ☐ Air
- ☐ Bush
- ☐ Feeder
- ☐ Other_____

BEAK SHAPE
- ☐ Hooked
- ☐ Cone
- ☐ Pointy
- ☐ Flat
- ☐ Long
- ☐ Other_____

TAIL
- ☐ Short
- ☐ Long
- ☐ Straight
- ☐ Fanned
- ☐ Forked
- ☐ Other_____

WINGS SHAPE
- ☐ Short
- ☐ Long
- ☐ Pointy
- ☐ Broad
- ☐ Round
- ☐ Other_____

MARKINGS & COLORS

_____

_____

_____

_____

WHAT IS THE BIRD DOING?	DID THE BIRD SING?
_____ _____	☐ Yes ☐ No

OTHER INTERESTING THINGS I NOTICED

_____

_____

_____

_____

_____

_____

PHOTO / SKETCH

BIRD WATCHING JOURNAL

DATE:	TIME:

WEATHER: ☀️🌤️☁️⛅🌧️⛈️🌙❄️ **SEASON:** 🌸 ☀️ 🍂 ❄️

LOCATION:

BIRD NAME:	BIRD TYPE:

HOW MANY DID YOU SEE?

1   2   3   4   5   6   7   8+

HOW BIG IS THE BIRD?

Tiny   Small   Medium   Big   Very Big

BIRD LOCATION
☐ Ground
☐ Tree
☐ Air
☐ Bush
☐ Feeder
☐ Other_____

BEAK SHAPE
☐ Hooked
☐ Cone
☐ Pointy
☐ Flat
☐ Long
☐ Other_____

TAIL
☐ Short
☐ Long
☐ Straight
☐ Fanned
☐ Forked
☐ Other_____

WINGS SHAPE
☐ Short
☐ Long
☐ Pointy
☐ Broad
☐ Round
☐ Other_____

MARKINGS & COLORS

_____
_____
_____
_____

WHAT IS THE BIRD DOING?

_____

_____

DID THE BIRD SING?

☐ Yes   ☐ No

OTHER INTERESTING THINGS I NOTICED

_____

_____

_____

_____

_____

_____

PHOTO / SKETCH

BIRD WATCHING JOURNAL

DATE:	TIME:
WEATHER:	SEASON:
LOCATION:	

BIRD NAME:	BIRD TYPE:
HOW MANY DID YOU SEE? 1 2 3 4 5 6 7 8+	**HOW BIG IS THE BIRD?** Tiny Small Medium Big Very Big

BIRD LOCATION
- ☐ Ground
- ☐ Tree
- ☐ Air
- ☐ Bush
- ☐ Feeder
- ☐ Other_____

BEAK SHAPE
- ☐ Hooked
- ☐ Cone
- ☐ Pointy
- ☐ Flat
- ☐ Long
- ☐ Other_____

TAIL
- ☐ Short
- ☐ Long
- ☐ Straight
- ☐ Fanned
- ☐ Forked
- ☐ Other_____

WINGS SHAPE
- ☐ Short
- ☐ Long
- ☐ Pointy
- ☐ Broad
- ☐ Round
- ☐ Other_____

MARKINGS & COLORS

_____

_____

_____

_____

WHAT IS THE BIRD DOING?

_____

_____

DID THE BIRD SING?

☐ Yes   ☐ No

OTHER INTERESTING THINGS I NOTICED

_____

_____

_____

_____

_____

_____

PHOTO / SKETCH

BIRD WATCHING JOURNAL

DATE:	TIME:
WEATHER: ☀☁☁⛅⛈🌧🌙❄	SEASON: ❀ ☀ 🍃 ❄
LOCATION:	

BIRD NAME:	BIRD TYPE:
HOW MANY DID YOU SEE? 1 2 3 4 5 6 7 8+	**HOW BIG IS THE BIRD?** Tiny Small Medium Big Very Big

BIRD LOCATION
- ☐ Ground
- ☐ Tree
- ☐ Air
- ☐ Bush
- ☐ Feeder
- ☐ Other_____

BEAK SHAPE
- ☐ Hooked
- ☐ Cone
- ☐ Pointy
- ☐ Flat
- ☐ Long
- ☐ Other_____

TAIL
- ☐ Short
- ☐ Long
- ☐ Straight
- ☐ Fanned
- ☐ Forked
- ☐ Other_____

WINGS SHAPE
- ☐ Short
- ☐ Long
- ☐ Pointy
- ☐ Broad
- ☐ Round
- ☐ Other_____

MARKINGS & COLORS

_____
_____
_____
_____

WHAT IS THE BIRD DOING?

_____

_____

DID THE BIRD SING?

☐ Yes   ☐ No

OTHER INTERESTING THINGS I NOTICED

_____

_____

_____

_____

_____

_____

PHOTO / SKETCH

BIRD WATCHING JOURNAL

DATE:	TIME:
WEATHER: ☀ ⛅ ☁ 🌧 ⛈ 🌙 ❄	SEASON: ❁ ☀ 🍂 ❄
LOCATION:	

BIRD NAME:	BIRD TYPE:
HOW MANY DID YOU SEE? 1 2 3 4 5 6 7 8+	**HOW BIG IS THE BIRD?** Tiny Small Medium Big Very Big

BIRD LOCATION
- ☐ Ground
- ☐ Tree
- ☐ Air
- ☐ Bush
- ☐ Feeder
- ☐ Other_____

BEAK SHAPE
- ☐ Hooked
- ☐ Cone
- ☐ Pointy
- ☐ Flat
- ☐ Long
- ☐ Other_____

TAIL
- ☐ Short
- ☐ Long
- ☐ Straight
- ☐ Fanned
- ☐ Forked
- ☐ Other_____

WINGS SHAPE
- ☐ Short
- ☐ Long
- ☐ Pointy
- ☐ Broad
- ☐ Round
- ☐ Other_____

MARKINGS & COLORS

_____

_____

_____

_____

WHAT IS THE BIRD DOING?

_____

_____

DID THE BIRD SING?

☐ Yes   ☐ No

OTHER INTERESTING THINGS I NOTICED

_____

_____

_____

_____

_____

_____

PHOTO / SKETCH

BIRD WATCHING JOURNAL

DATE:	TIME:

WEATHER: **SEASON:**

LOCATION:

BIRD NAME:	BIRD TYPE:

HOW MANY DID YOU SEE?

1   2   3   4   5   6   7   8+

HOW BIG IS THE BIRD?

Tiny   Small   Medium   Big   Very Big

BIRD LOCATION
- [ ] Ground
- [ ] Tree
- [ ] Air
- [ ] Bush
- [ ] Feeder
- [ ] Other_____

BEAK SHAPE
- [ ] Hooked
- [ ] Cone
- [ ] Pointy
- [ ] Flat
- [ ] Long
- [ ] Other_____

TAIL
- [ ] Short
- [ ] Long
- [ ] Straight
- [ ] Fanned
- [ ] Forked
- [ ] Other_____

WINGS SHAPE
- [ ] Short
- [ ] Long
- [ ] Pointy
- [ ] Broad
- [ ] Round
- [ ] Other_____

MARKINGS & COLORS

_____

_____

_____

_____

WHAT IS THE BIRD DOING?

_____

_____

DID THE BIRD SING?

☐ Yes ☐ No

OTHER INTERESTING THINGS I NOTICED

_____

_____

_____

_____

_____

_____

PHOTO / SKETCH

BIRD WATCHING JOURNAL

DATE:	TIME:
WEATHER: ☀️🌤️⛅🌧️⛈️🌙❄️	SEASON: ✿ ☀️ 🍃 ❄️
LOCATION:	

BIRD NAME:	BIRD TYPE:
HOW MANY DID YOU SEE? 1 2 3 4 5 6 7 8+	**HOW BIG IS THE BIRD?** Tiny Small Medium Big Very Big

BIRD LOCATION
- ☐ Ground
- ☐ Tree
- ☐ Air
- ☐ Bush
- ☐ Feeder
- ☐ Other_____

BEAK SHAPE
- ☐ Hooked
- ☐ Cone
- ☐ Pointy
- ☐ Flat
- ☐ Long
- ☐ Other_____

TAIL
- ☐ Short
- ☐ Long
- ☐ Straight
- ☐ Fanned
- ☐ Forked
- ☐ Other_____

WINGS SHAPE
- ☐ Short
- ☐ Long
- ☐ Pointy
- ☐ Broad
- ☐ Round
- ☐ Other_____

MARKINGS & COLORS
_____
_____
_____
_____

WHAT IS THE BIRD DOING?

_____

_____

DID THE BIRD SING?

☐ Yes ☐ No

OTHER INTERESTING THINGS I NOTICED

_____

_____

_____

_____

_____

_____

PHOTO / SKETCH

BIRD WATCHING JOURNAL

DATE:	TIME:
WEATHER: ☀☁⛅☁🌧⛈🌙❄	SEASON: ✿ ☀ 🍂 ❄
LOCATION:	

BIRD NAME:	BIRD TYPE:
HOW MANY DID YOU SEE? 1 2 3 4 5 6 7 8+	**HOW BIG IS THE BIRD?** Tiny Small Medium Big Very Big

BIRD LOCATION
- [ ] Ground
- [ ] Tree
- [ ] Air
- [ ] Bush
- [ ] Feeder
- [ ] Other_____

BEAK SHAPE
- [ ] Hooked
- [ ] Cone
- [ ] Pointy
- [ ] Flat
- [ ] Long
- [ ] Other_____

TAIL
- [ ] Short
- [ ] Long
- [ ] Straight
- [ ] Fanned
- [ ] Forked
- [ ] Other_____

WINGS SHAPE
- [ ] Short
- [ ] Long
- [ ] Pointy
- [ ] Broad
- [ ] Round
- [ ] Other_____

MARKINGS & COLORS

_____

_____

_____

_____

WHAT IS THE BIRD DOING?

_____

_____

DID THE BIRD SING?

☐ Yes   ☐ No

OTHER INTERESTING THINGS I NOTICED

_____

_____

_____

_____

_____

_____

PHOTO / SKETCH

BIRD WATCHING JOURNAL

DATE:	TIME:
WEATHER:	SEASON:
LOCATION:	

BIRD NAME:	BIRD TYPE:
HOW MANY DID YOU SEE? 1 2 3 4 5 6 7 8+	**HOW BIG IS THE BIRD?** Tiny Small Medium Big Very Big

BIRD LOCATION
- ☐ Ground
- ☐ Tree
- ☐ Air
- ☐ Bush
- ☐ Feeder
- ☐ Other_____

BEAK SHAPE
- ☐ Hooked
- ☐ Cone
- ☐ Pointy
- ☐ Flat
- ☐ Long
- ☐ Other_____

TAIL
- ☐ Short
- ☐ Long
- ☐ Straight
- ☐ Fanned
- ☐ Forked
- ☐ Other_____

WINGS SHAPE
- ☐ Short
- ☐ Long
- ☐ Pointy
- ☐ Broad
- ☐ Round
- ☐ Other_____

MARKINGS & COLORS

_____

_____

_____

_____

WHAT IS THE BIRD DOING?

_____

_____

DID THE BIRD SING?

☐ Yes ☐ No

OTHER INTERESTING THINGS I NOTICED

_____

_____

_____

_____

_____

_____

PHOTO / SKETCH

BIRD WATCHING JOURNAL

DATE:	TIME:
WEATHER: ☀️🌤️⛅🌧️⛈️🌙❄️	SEASON: 🌸 ☀️ 🍃 ❄️
LOCATION:	

BIRD NAME:	BIRD TYPE:
HOW MANY DID YOU SEE? 1 2 3 4 5 6 7 8+	**HOW BIG IS THE BIRD?** Tiny Small Medium Big Very Big

BIRD LOCATION
☐ Ground
☐ Tree
☐ Air
☐ Bush
☐ Feeder
☐ Other_____

BEAK SHAPE
☐ Hooked
☐ Cone
☐ Pointy
☐ Flat
☐ Long
☐ Other_____

TAIL
☐ Short
☐ Long
☐ Straight
☐ Fanned
☐ Forked
☐ Other_____

WINGS SHAPE
☐ Short
☐ Long
☐ Pointy
☐ Broad
☐ Round
☐ Other_____

MARKINGS & COLORS

_____

_____

_____

_____

WHAT IS THE BIRD DOING?

_____

_____

DID THE BIRD SING?

☐ Yes ☐ No

OTHER INTERESTING THINGS I NOTICED

_____

_____

_____

_____

_____

_____

PHOTO / SKETCH

BIRD WATCHING JOURNAL

DATE:	TIME:
WEATHER: ☀☁☁☁☁☾❄	SEASON: ❀ ☀ 🍂 ❄
LOCATION:	

BIRD NAME:	BIRD TYPE:
HOW MANY DID YOU SEE? 1 2 3 4 5 6 7 8+	**HOW BIG IS THE BIRD?** Tiny Small Medium Big Very Big

BIRD LOCATION
- ☐ Ground
- ☐ Tree
- ☐ Air
- ☐ Bush
- ☐ Feeder
- ☐ Other_____

BEAK SHAPE
- ☐ Hooked
- ☐ Cone
- ☐ Pointy
- ☐ Flat
- ☐ Long
- ☐ Other_____

TAIL
- ☐ Short
- ☐ Long
- ☐ Straight
- ☐ Fanned
- ☐ Forked
- ☐ Other_____

WINGS SHAPE
- ☐ Short
- ☐ Long
- ☐ Pointy
- ☐ Broad
- ☐ Round
- ☐ Other_____

MARKINGS & COLORS
_____
_____
_____
_____

WHAT IS THE BIRD DOING?

_____

_____

DID THE BIRD SING?

☐ Yes ☐ No

OTHER INTERESTING THINGS I NOTICED

_____

_____

_____

_____

_____

_____

PHOTO / SKETCH

BIRD WATCHING JOURNAL

DATE:	TIME:
WEATHER:	SEASON:
LOCATION:	

BIRD NAME:	BIRD TYPE:
HOW MANY DID YOU SEE? 1 2 3 4 5 6 7 8+	**HOW BIG IS THE BIRD?** Tiny Small Medium Big Very Big

BIRD LOCATION
- [ ] Ground
- [ ] Tree
- [ ] Air
- [ ] Bush
- [ ] Feeder
- [ ] Other_____

BEAK SHAPE
- [ ] Hooked
- [ ] Cone
- [ ] Pointy
- [ ] Flat
- [ ] Long
- [ ] Other_____

TAIL
- [ ] Short
- [ ] Long
- [ ] Straight
- [ ] Fanned
- [ ] Forked
- [ ] Other_____

WINGS SHAPE
- [ ] Short
- [ ] Long
- [ ] Pointy
- [ ] Broad
- [ ] Round
- [ ] Other_____

MARKINGS & COLORS

_____

_____

_____

_____

WHAT IS THE BIRD DOING?

_____

_____

DID THE BIRD SING?

☐ Yes ☐ No

OTHER INTERESTING THINGS I NOTICED

_____

_____

_____

_____

_____

_____

PHOTO / SKETCH

BIRD WATCHING JOURNAL

DATE:	TIME:
WEATHER: ☀️🌤️⛅🌧️⛈️🌙❄️	SEASON: 🌸 ☀️ 🍂 ❄️
LOCATION:	

BIRD NAME:	BIRD TYPE:
HOW MANY DID YOU SEE? 1 2 3 4 5 6 7 8+	**HOW BIG IS THE BIRD?** Tiny Small Medium Big Very Big

BIRD LOCATION
- ☐ Ground
- ☐ Tree
- ☐ Air
- ☐ Bush
- ☐ Feeder
- ☐ Other_____

BEAK SHAPE
- ☐ Hooked
- ☐ Cone
- ☐ Pointy
- ☐ Flat
- ☐ Long
- ☐ Other_____

TAIL
- ☐ Short
- ☐ Long
- ☐ Straight
- ☐ Fanned
- ☐ Forked
- ☐ Other_____

WINGS SHAPE
- ☐ Short
- ☐ Long
- ☐ Pointy
- ☐ Broad
- ☐ Round
- ☐ Other_____

MARKINGS & COLORS

_____

_____

_____

_____

WHAT IS THE BIRD DOING?

_____

_____

DID THE BIRD SING?

☐ Yes   ☐ No

OTHER INTERESTING THINGS I NOTICED

_____

_____

_____

_____

_____

_____

PHOTO / SKETCH

BIRD WATCHING JOURNAL

DATE:	TIME:
WEATHER: ☀️🌤️☁️🌧️⛈️🌙❄️	SEASON: 🌸 ☀️ 🍂 ❄️
LOCATION:	

BIRD NAME:	BIRD TYPE:
HOW MANY DID YOU SEE? 1 2 3 4 5 6 7 8+	**HOW BIG IS THE BIRD?** Tiny Small Medium Big Very Big

BIRD LOCATION
- [ ] Ground
- [ ] Tree
- [ ] Air
- [ ] Bush
- [ ] Feeder
- [ ] Other_____

BEAK SHAPE
- [ ] Hooked
- [ ] Cone
- [ ] Pointy
- [ ] Flat
- [ ] Long
- [ ] Other_____

TAIL
- [ ] Short
- [ ] Long
- [ ] Straight
- [ ] Fanned
- [ ] Forked
- [ ] Other_____

WINGS SHAPE
- [ ] Short
- [ ] Long
- [ ] Pointy
- [ ] Broad
- [ ] Round
- [ ] Other_____

MARKINGS & COLORS

_____
_____
_____
_____

WHAT IS THE BIRD DOING?

_____

_____

DID THE BIRD SING?

☐ Yes   ☐ No

OTHER INTERESTING THINGS I NOTICED

_____

_____

_____

_____

_____

_____

PHOTO / SKETCH

BIRD WATCHING JOURNAL

DATE:

TIME:

WEATHER: ☀ ⛅ ☁ ⛈ 🌧 🌙 ❄

SEASON: ✿ ☀ 🍃 ❄

LOCATION:

BIRD NAME:

BIRD TYPE:

HOW MANY DID YOU SEE?

1   2   3   4   5   6   7   8+

HOW BIG IS THE BIRD?

Tiny   Small   Medium   Big   Very Big

BIRD LOCATION
- ☐ Ground
- ☐ Tree
- ☐ Air
- ☐ Bush
- ☐ Feeder
- ☐ Other_____

BEAK SHAPE
- ☐ Hooked
- ☐ Cone
- ☐ Pointy
- ☐ Flat
- ☐ Long
- ☐ Other_____

TAIL
- ☐ Short
- ☐ Long
- ☐ Straight
- ☐ Fanned
- ☐ Forked
- ☐ Other_____

WINGS SHAPE
- ☐ Short
- ☐ Long
- ☐ Pointy
- ☐ Broad
- ☐ Round
- ☐ Other_____

MARKINGS & COLORS

_____

_____

_____

_____

WHAT IS THE BIRD DOING?

_____

_____

DID THE BIRD SING?

☐ Yes   ☐ No

OTHER INTERESTING THINGS I NOTICED

_____

_____

_____

_____

_____

_____

PHOTO / SKETCH

KINGFISHER

HUMMINGBIRD

MACAW

OWL

CARDINAL

COCKATOO

TURKEY

TOUCAN

COCKATIEL

BLUE JAY

THANK YOU FOR YOUR PURCHASE!

If you enjoyed this book, please consider taking a moment to leave an honest review. Your feedback is important to us as we strive to improve the quality and value of our work. If you have any questions, suggestions, or concerns please do not hesitate to contact us at cleverkidpress@gmail.com or via our website at www.CleverKidPress.com. Thanks!

Printed in Great Britain
by Amazon